About Those Losses

Poems by James Benger,
Sarah Worrel and Lindsey Martin-Bowen

Spartan
Press

Spartan Press
Kansas City, Missouri

Spartan
Press

Copyright © James Benger, Sarah Worrel,
Lindsey Martin-Bowen, 2024
First Edition: 1 3 5 7 9 10 8 6 4 2
ISBN: 978-1-958182-90-1
LCCN: 2024946153

Cover image: Mike Labrum
Author photos: David Arnold Hughes, Jeremey Worrel,
Nellie Sudbrock

Table of Contents:

Dedicated to all who've suffered a loss,
no matter the magnitude, for even the losses
some may deem minor can shatter another's reality.

...it is loss to which everything flows,
absence in which everything flowers.

- Margaret Atwood

About Those Losses

Mariah

lived down the cul-de-sac at
the end of the bulb

she freaked at the sight of
blood when she got cut on our old
swingset
the blue-and-white metal one

I had read an explicit romance novel at
Kendra's house and I
tried
to make sense of it with
Mariah but it was too much

then I stole her rings and I
felt guilty for years
so when she was passing messages for
the office in one of my classes I
brought them and tried to give
them back but she wouldn't take them the
first time and didn't want to take them the
second time but she did

-Sarah Worrel

lost division

we would pedal our bikes
trudging the gravel that was mostly dust
of marquette ave
squat boxes and single wides

that one weird kid's parents
kept a donkey in the pen out back
and chickens that would
scatter at a call of "shitters!"

that stray dog always following
waiting for someone to drop something
waiting for someone to drop

there was the weird dude
in the tarpaper shack on the edge of the woods
who never came out
but to put empties on the porch
and shoo any of us away
who were brave enough to snoop

we were looking for anything
under those endless sycamores
we knew something had been lost
years ago
decades ago
and the trees
the road
the houses

the families
were still trying to figure out
what was missing

and we were just young enough
to be naïve and bold enough
to think we could save the world

if you followed the gravel and dirt long enough
you'd end up on pavement

THE SUBDIVISION

we always said it in reverent capitals
because that's the place where it hadn't been lost
not all of it at least
not yet
there the patchy grass was still kind of green
and there were a few
honest to god real basketball hoops in driveways
not the metal rings nailed to trees back our way
we marveled at how a kid might skateboard
were they so inclined

and we convinced the one boy to get his parents
to give us the scrap wood in their backyard
and we cobbled a bike ramp
in the field just south of

THE SUBDIVISION

we rode that ramp the whole summer
gravel kids and pavement kids together
and no one laughed when someone bled
and someone's mom always had kool aid
when it got too hot

and when we pedaled back to our
lot of dust and dirt
shutting drafty front doors
and closing our eyes
something had been found

-James Benger

Kendra

had a younger
brother and a cute older
one who almost wrecked
my bike once
because I
parked it in the driveway behind
his car

he brought it inside
yelling at me so the next
time I went over I
locked my bike up in the middle
of their yard to the lonely tree

she guzzled
sodas
without ever
drinking water

gave up her virginity to
the neighborhood bully for
two cigarettes which I always thought
was cool but
later she told me that
it made her feel
like a whore

-Sarah Worrel

trickle down

little drummer boy roy's little sister
regularly ragged on the upperclassmen
especially those in
their cousin's hand me downs
windbreakers and jeans and starter jackets
that were last popular
when king george the first
was still mind wanking about the presidency

and i never understood where she got off
seeing as she wasn't cute
or funny
or really a nice person
and her older brother
nor their parents
seemed to give much of a shake about her

but then
maybe that last part
was all the answer needed

-James Benger

Lisa

dated John who fucked
anything female that moved

even Jane with the
back hair that he said
he didn't want to screw

and Maddox and I hung out in
the garage while John
fucked her and I'm pretty
sure Lisa & John were broken
up by then or I'd have
been freaking out

but John was always
grabbing or itching his
junk and it was no
surprise when he gave
crotch rot to Lisa
and her mom was equally
fucked up – probably why
Lisa was dating John – he
wasn't good enough for
her

but one night she paged me
and I called her
I had school and work the
next day

but her mom had thrown
her dresser drawers and
contents down the
stairs and Lisa asked for
help but I was an ass
and said no

then I couldn't sleep
anyway – I should have
gone

-Sarah Worrel

m

when we met
he was living with his cousin
at the end of the hall

i tried to take his side
on everything
but he was always
so angry
then again
i suppose that'll happen
if your mom
shoots herself in the head
from the park bench
while you're tossing a frisbee

we got drunk a lot
talked music and movies
he dug goth metal and
horror flicks
i was more into grunge and
arthouse stuff
one night a case of red stripe in
he tried to sell me on the
artistic merit of
manson's golden age of grotesque and
freddy vs jason
i equally tried to convince him of that
peach gb album and
sideways

we did a lot of wobbly agreeing to disagree

after his cousin got tired of it all
he got a room in a duplex with some dude
way older and much more mature than us
then there was that big party
where i passed out on the floor
and someone pissed on the rug
and someone else
broke their arm out on the deck
and that was that

he moved somewhere else
only saw him once after that
he'd shaved his head
met a girl with a shaved head
seemed good

-James Benger

It's never like the movies—

for my father

this dying: no background chords
rising to a crescendo,
no adagio of strings.
You watch these ants, instead,
trickle across peonies.
They disappear. And you
can't keep your grip
on that granite wall of reason
but slip downstream
into some wild current
till you run aground.
There, you search
for the deserted place, a Holy Land,
where Elijah met God.
Even if you're hiking
the Appalachian Trail, up
Standing Indian Mountain,
you watch vultures circle
in and out of clouds festering
into some murky, yellow soup.
And when lightning hits,
Father Davis says Hail Marys—
and there, on the horizon,
you see Wovoka whirl
in his dance of ghosts.

-Lindsey Martin-Bowen

She

was dying
and I couldn't even
call her

it was too
hard

you could talk to her in
the spring for only 20
minutes before she would
get confused and ask
the same question about
coronavirus she'd
asked at the
start

and it
hurt to
talk to her
like that

so I was
a coward

and I didn't even
call her for six
months

she died six
days ago
and the grief
is so fresh

I can't even
write this
without crying
normally I
wait until
the feelings
fade but
these are raw
and horrid
and I hate
feeling weak

I hate crying in
front of other
people
on
display
like some kind of animal

her body
fuck

I had to walk up
to it to even see the
funeral parlor had
the right woman

the toughest broad I
have ever known was
gone and the thing in
the casket had the right
cheekbones and jawline and no
eyeglasses so
the thing didn't look
like her
the makeup was more than
she ever wore in life and
it flaked and looked
like shit

but my grandma wasn't
there

she was
already
gone

and I got to
parade my pain
in front of
others at
her funeral
as if I had
a choice

it was another
command performance
just like every other
family event I've
ever gone to

if I'd had
my way
I'd have stayed
home to mourn her in
private
and kept my
weakness to
myself

so last night I
dreamed I was
avoiding her
again

still

-Sarah Worrel

2000

it was no news
that she was on her way out
had been most of our lives
slowly trickling away
one organ scooped out at a time
sections replaced with
plastic tubes and whatnot

and she started wearing that beanie
because there wasn't much
going on underneath
and that never bothered me
but the fake breasts
the plastic things she wore
when going out
seemed so unnecessary and wrong

but she almost never cried
and never let the kids
really know what was going on
as she walked them the
mile and a half to baskin robbins
toting her chemo box all the while
hose sticking into a port
less than expertly hidden under her shirt

and it wasn't until the night at the
little kids softball game
when she couldn't hold her scant dinner

creamed corn between her feet
below the rusting bleachers
and i drove her home in a dying station wagon
her husband once owned

i drove her to our couch
then rushed back to the diamond
to pick up the rest after the game
but the streetlights swam in my vision
and somewhere i knew
i'd only see her a few more times

and she died one day
far away in a shack in kentucky
while i was laid up in a fold out bed
with a rolled convertible crunched up spine
and that's how the century started

-James Benger

Since You Left

to my mother

My plants refuse to speak to me.
I drag around a silent household,
listen for your words in each room,
and shuffle past an empty table.
There, morning sunlight glints
off that spot where yesterday,
you left your glasses.

Today, smells of dying roses
linger, and light spreads across
the wall, unlike last night,
when candlelight carved shadows
deep as your eyes while you exhaled
one last breath. Your moans of pain
became too intense for words.

But now I miss those groans
when I hear nothing—no
sounds, except the thuds
of the water heater
and the thunder
of the furnace
firing its last.

-Lindsey Martin-Bowen

The Serenity Prayer

was introduced to me long before I
had a need for it

always having done church and thinking
I had a great relationship with the ol' JC
but in all seriousness
I cling to my Christian God and
then I run away

and I found myself sitting
in a meeting
however many years later
reciting the Serenity Prayer

God grant me
the serenity to accept
the things I
cannot change
the courage to change
the things I can and
the wisdom to
know the difference (and
accept
the rest)

so I couldn't even
pray the prayer when I
first got to meetings because
I didn't mean it

I couldn't pray a liturgy with
others

I had to start
letting go
of a lot of
fucking baggage

one small toiletry
bag at a fucking time

and to let go of the anger
the bitterness
the wrath
and I thought I was doing
so well on the prescription
drugs and dealing with
the depression

but I was so
wrong

and yesterday I was going
through my luggage

tidying under my bed
and I found pictures
of the whole reason I was
in S-Anon to begin with

and I didn't snoop
I didn't go looking for

more evidence of what I'd
already known in my heart

didn't neglect my child
as I looked for that
evidence

because the crazy train
has left the premises and
I'm on the right
meds
now

-Sarah Worrel

liturgy

never had much need
for the congregating together
in some building
while a guy who didn't know you
shouted about how you're going to hell
if you didn't come back
every weekend
and get kneebound
and give up every ounce of your
hard won self possession

the church down the gravel road
felt like little more
than a modified trailer
and the gravel was always
denser and whiter
than the street
or anyone's driveways
and i always felt that said more
about the state of things
than i ever could

so we rode our bikes past it
and wondered
why
why
why
because if there was some kind of deity
it surely wasn't in that
pristine little building

it was in the leaves high above
or the clouds
or the mud between toes
as the post rain shower worms
wriggled their way up to the sun

so if ever we were to pray
it was to the rotting box turtle in the woods
the coyote skull
the image of the bluegill
just before its spine was severed

some sweltering summer afternoons
i'd pedal to rose lawn
sit at his grave
and wonder if he ever had those thoughts
i saw how his blade moved
once upon a bye
and i think
maybe he did

-James Benger

Bonsai Tree Gone Awry

Before he died, Father
worked in the shadows, welding
pipes into a multi-pointed star
Shaped like an off-kilter Bonsai
in the back yard.
Today, a helicopter circles

a sawed-off pine, and
brown needles scatter into grass
and onto a patio.
I sweep them off—
stare at the huge steel vulture
and smell mold when I water the roses,

those flowers of funerals and wakes.
The chopper dips lower,
as if it might land on the concrete.
I try to pretend brushing away leaves
will bring an early spring.
I sweep till my wrist aches.

The noise of the chopper grows louder
and I squint at the rusty sculpture
in the garden. Mother never liked it
perhaps because it points to the sky,
the heavens, to every direction
but home.

-Lindsey Martin-Bowen

thanksgiving 1998

there was that november
when we were prepping to move
to the other side of the midwest
leaving everything i'd ever known
family
friends
job
headshop

mom said what with all that
she wasn't about to
fuck with having to cook thanksgiving

so we did it at grandma's place
cramped one bedroom
from the mid 1800s
dirt floor basement
hand pump for chunky yellow water
out in the yard

year before grandma conned her husband
to take out a loan
update the kitchen from its
1930s accoutrements to
something a little more modern
a 70s kitchen outfit she found
at an estate sale

grandpa kept all the old stuff
loaded it into one of his barns
ran a rigged gas line
a water line that dumped
into the creek at the property's edge

while grandma fretted in her kitchen
bounced into the living room
to fiddle with the rabbit ears
so the kids would be entertained
grandpa slow cooked the turkey
surrounded by silence
five gallon buckets of broken faucets
and an industrial tiller
he hadn't had the energy to push in years

every now and then
he'd lift from the plastic lawn chair
make for the beer shed
he had a lot of barns and sheds
so naturally one was devoted to beer
come back with a can of miller
return to his quietude

that day was twenty three years ago today
grandpa had less than five years left
grandma had less than ten
mom had just under eleven

thanksgiving morning
i drink coffee and type this
my sons grin and dance around
their table of toys

i get a sideview of their faces
the mischievous smirks remind me
of how grandpa would
dance around the kitchen table
flaunting his ill gotten victory
after cheating at a round of rummy

it gives me a smile
imagining grandpa somewhere
sitting in a lawn chair
as a bird slow roasts
watching all of this from a
smudged barn window
and cracking another can

-James Benger

Easter morning

on the way to church
and smoke starts billowing from the vents
so Mom pulls over by the Amos Family Funeral Home
off of I-35 and Mom sends my brother and I to church
with near-strangers

I hear later that the Dodge Aries station wagon
burned so fiercely the firefighters thought it might explode
and looking at pictures later
you can see the keys melted off the key ring

-Sarah Worrel

September Fires

In memory of Diane Wahto
(January 24, 1940-September 16, 2020)

The dawn comes late now. Clouds mix with smoke
    particulates—
plastics from burnt out-towns—to blot out the sun—
    till the smoke's
more toxic than fumes from forest fires. More deadly.

The haze blew in from California and Oregon, across
    plains
to your Wichita home. But you won't see it or inhale it,
    even if the
jet stream rushes it there. You left that city yesterday.
    Instead,

in Lake Huron, you swim an Australian crawl you learned
    as a girl.
Pulling through cold, gray water without a ripple, you
    squint at a distant,
sandy shore. Once you left that lake to return to birch
    trees, your Kansas

suburban home, husband, children, and your dog Annie,
    who
scampered through your poems. No transparent fish or
    aquatic
plants here. Oaks, birches, and pines. And I recall so many

of your words sent *via* an electric connection. They haunt
  me still

on the other side of the continent, where I sit amid smoke.
  And

a charcoal spirit surrounds me. Black pine needles prick
  my hands.

-Lindsey Martin-Bowen

I had to

reread "She"
and realize that the woman
I adored
was truly gone
long before I had
to look at that thing
in the coffin
and parade my
pain
in front of
others

I didn't know
Diane
but I wish I
had
I wonder if she
was at the Watkins
Museum reading we
all did a few years
back
but my failed memory
betrays me
again

and I don't
know
if it's the booze
or peri-menopause

or food intolerance
brain fog
or what the fuck
is wrong with
me

and I don't
know how other
people don't
see what a complete
fucking fraud I
am

always
pretending like I
have my shit together

so cliché, right?

and I know
that no one else
does either
but some days
it's all I can do
to put on my
war paint
(black eyeliner)
and fix my girl
mohawk
so I
can face anyone
and everyone

and other days the meds
work and I feel
fine
which I haven't felt for
most of a decade
and mental illness stole
that time from me and I
will never get it
back

just like dementia stole
the toughest broad I've
ever known
long before
I had to see the thing
in the coffin

and the God I
thought I knew
was loving
and merciful
so why
do we all have
to live through
so much
loss?

so I can
pretend like I
know I'm going to
see that tough broad
again

but I don't know any
more anything than
anyone else on this
cursed planet

so all I can
do is pretend I
still
believe
and pretend that
it is solace
enough

-Sarah Worrel

for Diane

and now that you've left us
for whatever else there is
we wonder how and why

but those are unfair questions
one has only to
look and know the answers

yours was the pinnacle
of a life well lived
maximum impact
the sweetest razor
hidden in the flowers

i imagine you being
flattered but embarrassed
by all of this

but it's your show
it always was

-James Benger

It Isn't Like the Opera, Either
(Companion Piece to "It's Never Like the Movies")

for Ruth Bader Ginsburg

(March 15, 1933-September 18, 2020)

this slow ebbing away—
not like Tosca leaping
off a parapet
to her death—

or a corundum-colored
clash of swords in
a duel ending
a wild conundrum.

Instead, you
step into a woods
after the sun slips
behind cliffs,

and pine needles
hover, turning
paths dark.
You tiptoe

across thin grass
around stones
and coves where
toadstools bark

in voices creating
choruses Handel
might have woven
into a new *Messiah*.

-Lindsey Martin-Bowen

And it isn't like my childhood

the childhood
my daughter
gets

I don't remember her
ever building
a fort

like my brother
and I
did

and I can't
remember
if my sister
did too
or if she was
too little

we'd build in
the basement
of the old
house
my brother and I

with cushions
from the corduroy
couch
and sheets—

I can't remember
which ones

but my mom didn't
yell
so we must have
asked

or we'd build a
fort under
the dining room
table

but the basement
was my favorite
and I had this
puffy
pink
wallet
that I loved

before I
decided I
was done
with
pink
and
lace
and
all
things
reeking

of
girliness

and I
still
wish I
had that
damn
wallet

because I
seem to
remember
that it
had a
character
on the front
but I couldn't
say which
character

and this loss
is one
too many

and I
want my
damn
pink
wallet
back to
see if I

even
remember
that
right

and I
remember
playing soldiers
with my brother
and the two
boys from
next door
and how
I threw a
plastic machine
gun over the
fence and
one of the boys
had to get
stitches
because I
threw it
blindly
and it was
a bloody
head wound

and I was
probably wearing
that olive
green shirt
with the

embroidery in
the same color
that felt
like a
camouflaged war
shirt for
a girl

there were
no pine needles
in my parents'
front yard
but there was
thin grass
and lava rocks
and enough trees
we could pretend
were woods

but I was never
going to be
a soldier
like my dad
and serve
overseas

and I wonder
what my daughter
will make of this
depression
and what she
will carry with

her through
life
that isn't
really hers
to carry

and I
wish I
could bequeath
her with
memories of
siblings
and forts

but I will
never have
another child
with the meds
I'm on

and some days
that's okay
and on other
days it's a
fresh wound
and a
disappointment
all over
again

-Sarah Worrel

things we do

dad lived in antarctica for a while
always said how boring it was
once you got over the beauty of it all
it was just that thing he did that one time

after you hit that point there wasn't
much to do but get drunk
box penguins and screw with seagulls

he'd say you'd down a bottle
of jack and head to the junkyard
apparently there's a junkyard there
instead of a guard dog there was
the world's largest
perhaps an exaggeration
emperor penguin
many a besotted sailor was laid
out on the snow by the
massive black flipper

there's a movie theater but
the only film they had
remember this was the early seventies
was the sound of music
not the flick of choice for a bunch
of drunken homesick gi s whose
families were at home starving and
whose friends were over in viet nam
the reels made it into the snow
and then pissed on more than once

dad's got a million of these stories
funny enough they all take place at
a time when he was over a decade
younger than i am now

i wonder if i'll ever have stories so good
or if i missed my chance
it occurs to me that maybe dad's
never thought of any of these stories
as anything all that astounding

so maybe if i ever tell my sons about
the time i stowed away on a train
in france because i couldn't afford
the ticket back to paris and when i
got there i didn't have the ticket
to get into the airport and the
armed guard chased me but i lost
him only to find that i'd missed my
flight so i spent my last euro to call
my boss and say i wasn't going to
be in tomorrow and i slept under
an abandoned check in desk
with my jacket as a pillow while
i tried to figure out how the hell
i was going to get home

maybe they'll think it's pretty cool
to me it's just that thing i did
that one time

                              -James Benger

How You Dull the Pain
Under this Silent Canopy

to Jim Morrison

In memory of James Tate (December 8, 1943-July 8, 2015)

Sometimes I suffer with it, too, this slow burn
spreading into tributaries in the chest—yet
alcohol's a temporary solution working best

with much dilution—Communion wine,
half water—one sip or two—goes down
far more smoothly, keeps the mind less woozy.

You claim love's mainly pain. I say those who love
us most don't always treat us right. Yet because they
often do, they set us adrift with skewed aspirations.

Here, under Caribbean skies, a penguin leads her
brood through tall grasses where cockatiels fly and
alight on branches. The arctic birds dart around

snakes performing deadly dances. They take
jagged steps, toes turned inward, whirling
away from vipers until the birds almost keel.

Most penguins don't dig this hot aquatic scene
with thick palms instead of evergreens under skies
flat as blue paint inside a Victorian canopy for a royal

wedding. And smells of poi and hot spices don't do
their bills justice. They prefer salmon from icy seas,
where they swim and dive deep—far from a glowering sun.

Tonight, they'll try not to stink when they soak their feet
in Epsom-salt water, sip a pear drink, and seek out a sailor
to help them find a ball of cheese, the perfect ball of Cheese.

And I wonder if those young birds, like me, will learn
to protect themselves. I gleaned I'm a moth, drawn to
that which might—at any moment—burst me into flames..

-Lindsey Martin-Bowen

We Lost the Basement

and the house on Lower Beaver Road
long before we lost Grandma and Grandpa

the mighty trees with their acorns
that gave cool shade on the hottest days
and if I picked enough acorns
I'd earn a buck—
a quarter at a time

the basement was
always my favorite because it held
all the mysteries of life

my grandparents' old
motorcycle jackets in pleather
and the barrel of nuts with its
nutcracker

the shower stall that had to
be wiped down every time or
mildew would creep in

the fridge or freezer or both with
Hawkeye or Jello pudding pops
for a delicious treat any time we
visited

Grandma would make me
eggs, rice, and cheese

no matter the hour
and we'd watch the bird feeder in
the backyard from the kitchen
sink and Grandma could tell me
what kind each bird was

but I can't tell an oriole from
a meadowlark, my own state
bird

and I will never be able
to live up to her legacy
of the spic-and-span
home

-Sarah Worrel

cherry

there was a white cherry tree
out by the side of the
walled in screened in porch
back before it was walled in
and was just a screened in porch

the tree sprouted precariously
from the incline of a drainage ditch
that doubled as a property line

thorny roses overtook
the trestle on that end of the house
eventually going all
manifest destiny on the
peeling yellow siding

the way the tree was positioned
it was impossible to get any fruit
without also sinking deep into mud
the earth mixing with
brown water of questionable origin

the neighbor's great dane often
got to the low hanging cherries first
leaving us to attempt to climb
muddy boots skidding on flaking bark
callused hands on wet leaves

if you made it to the last sturdy
crotch in the tree
you could spend the rest of the sunlight
sucking on yellow fruit
spitting pits into the tricking brown ditch
and watching the sky turn red through the leaves

-James Benger

Erasures

Some one's erasing my life—
the bungalow where I was born.
The château where I birthed my daughter.
The Cape Cod where I raised my son—
all gone.

Turquoise ponds we skinny dipped,
hot clay shores where we unearthed clams.
No more. Only hot winds there—
no more cattails and cottages or cows
roaming free.

No map shows the cabins on the lake
where we boated and water skied,
as if our lives would roll on and on—
No more willows, waters on shores, ebbing
and flowing.

We howl at the moon, then slip away—
follow shadows into black spaces.
We're lunatics who've lost direction,
spinning like my cat with an aneurism—
also gone.

And They expect us to march uphill,
act courageous about our futures—
winners of a nation—when They
block out our victories, our memories,
our past.

-Lindsey Martin-Bowen

jackie

jackie lived in the run to hell
trailer on the other side of
the box wire fence
we rode the bus together

after school we'd toss my
rock solid basketball
back and forth over the fence

he never asked me to come over
said his mom didn't allow
people in her house

i always assumed jackie's mom worked a lot
i almost never saw her
now i wonder if maybe it had more
to do with those big men with
long beards and leather vests
that rode the thunderous motorcycles
and left empty aluminum cans
and broken needles all along the street

once when i was brushing my teeth
for bed i could hear the big men
making lots of noise from the
trailer next door
the occasional gunshot

jackie's mom didn't use the knocker
just pounded fists on the front door
i opened it white foam still around
my grade school mouth
she said she needed to use the phone

the cops came quick
bright flashes in that summer dark
jackie didn't talk much after that night

a few weeks later while
passing the basketball
i asked if he wanted to trade toys

jackie held the petrified
basketball to his chest and told me
i ain't got no toys
i ain't got nothin

then his mom called him in
a week later they were gone

the big loud men took over the
trailer for a while until the
city had it condemned and
hauled off

i wonder if jackie's still out there
if he remembers me
if so i'd want him to know
that i thought of him today

-James Benger

How stupid I was being

1976 Oldsmobile Cutlass Supreme V8
so much fun to drive

got to borrow it a few times
before Dad wrecked it on the highway

once I raced another car up Mur-Len
before I realized how fast I was going
how stupid I was being
like the kids we used to hear on 151st Street at night

-Sarah Worrel

County Fair Ferris Wheel Ride

To Ashe, my granddaughter

First revolutions
are the hardest: The wheel stops
when we're locked on top.
Winds swing our car, hard and far.
I fear we'll topple over.

Your mother shoots us
swinging aloft—my face cross-
looking as if mad—
angry. I wasn't—just scared,
unlike you who flew up here.

Below, some unload,
And the machine moves again,
this time without stops.
No rocking makes my heart race.
Your face morphs this into fun.

-Lindsey Martin-Bowen

Before our sister came along

One summer my brother and I
stayed with dad's parents and our cousin

I slept in the same
room with our cousin who
liked to fall asleep to a
radio when I was used to
silence

and we all got to go to
Adventureland
and it seems that Grandma and Grandpa
should have been there but I don't
remember that

I remember being in the car in the
morning as we were leaving and
realizing I didn't have any sunscreen and
none of the adults were going to scrounge any

buying trashy souvenirs and
earning a whopper of a lobster-red
sunburn and how there was no
air conditioning to help me feel
cooler

and how much it hurt to have
anything touching and I'd worn
a tank top with spaghetti straps and
how all of my other shirts had more

and I still don't remember how I
managed or if I borrowed
a shirt from my cousin or Grandma
or what I did

and I hardly remember my brother
being there at all except for
stories later about how Grandpa
didn't believe my brother took a
thorough shower in three minutes
and if I remember correctly—big if
Grandpa
helped my brother clean up when
it was absolutely unnecessary

-Sarah Worrel

christmas 1994

mom could make some eggnog
must've been two bottles of brandy
for every punchbowl
saran wrapped in the fridge
and all i wanted for christmas was
pulp fiction on vhs
and nirvana unplugged in new york on cassette

i got the movie but not the album
but that was okay
cause i had one friend whose parents
always tried to buy his love
so he was sure to get a cd player
with a tape deck
and i could supply a blank memorex

my cousin and i
we'd been filching nips of nog all day
but after dinner we got booze bold
filled a simpsons water bottle
took it to the basement
played my sega
i think it was nba jam
until we were too swervy to focus

then we popped the tape in
finished off the nog as projecting from a
twelve inch black and white tv
ving rhames said he was
pretty fuckin far from okay

-James Benger

After Reading "Saudade" by Erika L. Sánchez

You say you live in the Republic of Flowers.
I live in the Republic of Broccoli,
where I learn to fry skirts with frilly
words that mean everything
to those awake during wee hours,
scrubbing blood off floors or walls
after vampires break mirrors
that reflect too much sun.
I cannot bow to the authority
of flowers. I must bow
to the authority of vegetables,
or I'll become vulnerable as Mary Lu,
the girl local roofers raped inside a pool hall,
where they spread her like Indian Paintbrush
plucked from tundra surrounding
a mountain town. There, contractors,
carpenters, and workmen keep women
locked inside bedrooms.
    I need to survive in the city.
I'm scared when I inhale
scents from moldy limestone walls
circling Chicago or Miami,
wherever immigrants enter,
and the Man jots their names
onto lists he sends to the Asp
who executes them before they commit
crimes or marry citizens who turn them
into parts of us as we stroll
between two lions at the edge of a lagoon,

where swans circle each other
then dip into green water
and perform for the peacocks
on the shore, as if this were before
the second World War—
before Europe shivered
with news from Germany—
that second fall from grace.

-Lindsey Martin-Bowen

Lilac air freshener

in the bathroom at the
grandparents' house
ruined
the scent of lilac bushes for
me
forever
because now I can only
smell lilacs and shit

almost the same way that
I smell oranges and shit
from the air freshener
at the gas station on 135th St.

and the onyx nightmares of
working at the gas station
still haunt me
almost two
decades later

-Sarah Worrel

chuck taylors

we had endless summer moments
embraced in the pheromonal thrill of it all
nights when blue gave way only to green
and everything rolled sweet in the hills

rusted billboard poles and
busted no trespassing placards meant nothing
to midnight abandon

and our thin wallets grew thinner
on the lust of adventure

there is a smell of the air
around a gas pump at two am
when you're sixteen and have
nowhere
no one
to be
it smells like the memories that will be buried
until one chance day they're not
and the blood will boil again
in the sweet simmer of freedom

keys turned easy in ignitions
and secrets were locked away in the trunk
the backseat cried for more
and the sunrise on the horizon
always looked its most beautiful
through a cracked windshield

-James Benger

Persephone Waits
at the Hades Intersection

Each fall, he drags me here,
pulls me away from perfumed
pillows, sunlit rooms,
and city lights that flicker
not far from my window.

I miss strolling to the market,
where I finger pomegranates—
sipping coffee in a café,
and munching baklava
at afternoon tea.

Here, traffic shoves me to the curb,
splashes me with black water.
I wheel over asphalt, dodge semis
and SUVs, while I'm locked
inside a hot metal box.

-Lindsey Martin-Bowen

I always suspected

he would be an
excellent father
but I never expected how
much it would hurt to
see him father
another woman's children
he was supposed to
be mine

but when I
laid bare my
heart
he returned it
unwanted
and it's been
over a year now
but my heart still
aches at the idea of what I
could have had with
my Antony—
now hers

-Sarah Worrel

slow inferno

moving in circles
about one another's
circles,
life fails to compare
to the hollywood promise
of an absolute.

every day a near miss
every day a horseshoe
all of those days
may eventually add up
to a hand grenade.

-James Benger

Immortal Beloved—
Star-Crossed Once More

I search Pleiades
tonight, much like Ludwig sought
his beloved, a
star-crossed Romeo come too
late—Juliet departed

to another fate
without him. Like star showers,
they couldn't merge sparks
but spread apart. Missing one
connection glimmering a

line to the north star,
they throb for one beat. We, too,
struggle for that link.
From our porch, we watch the skies
and wait until morning comes,

when we'll go at it
again—never win this fight.
Words out-of-kilter
fail to connect star wishes—
each horizon sinks them all.

-Lindsey Martin-Bowen

Two nights ago

I dreamt of
my Antony

who I haven't
seen for
two years

and my heart
no longer
aches

-Sarah Worrel

even now

i'll see you

walking around the
trailer of a stalled big rig

cashing in your scratchers
ahead of me as i wait to
pay for a tank

banging broken pipes
on an overturned bucket
on the streetcorner for pennies

sitting at the bus stop
shedding the world
one hopeless shrug at a time
i'll see you doing these things
then you turn

and i remember
all the decades past
and the dirt still there
and you're still gone

-James Benger

Truckdriver's wife

It's midnight.
Maybe he's doin' a run
to Shaky Town

where some
lot lizard
checks his dip stick.

If he don't turn on his dog.
some bear'll nab him,
sure enough,

'fore he heads back to Windy,
where chains nick asphalt,
and I shiver at a window.

-Lindsey Martin-Bowen

Out the window

snow covers the neighborhood

I gear up to go outside
and I remember a pair of mittens
held together by a string

and I remember playing out in the cold for hours
but I wonder if I really remember the mittens
or if they ever existed at all

-Sarah Worrel

chew

he had a million stories
always flowing from nowhere
to envelope us in rhythmic
tones of tall tales spun as truth

in between sentences he'd pause
long enough to spit thin brown juice
into a gallon ice cream bucket
filled with sawdust

he never wore a shirt and he used
the same red bandana to wipe sweat
from his face and to blow his nose

he got around with a cane that was
only a glorified stick and when he
could no longer step up into his truck
he traded it in for a decade old
station wagon complete with
rust and slashed seats and an a m radio

the last time i saw him we stood
in the gravel driveway on a warm december
he gave me a cheap watch he'd found and
fixed and he offered me a pinch from the
pouch he kept in the glove compartment

i'm not sure of the last story he told me
but it's safe to say it was dirty and

told through a mouthful of
dentures and redman

he probably wouldn't
mind being remembered like that

                    -James Benger

Mary Todd Lincoln's Obsession

If she could find just the right pair—
white lacey ones, maybe, or the suede—
not too stiff, but soft enough
with smells of sweet perfume,
they'll smooth her rough knuckles
and reverse this streak of bad luck.

She understands how this universe
revolves in cycles. It moves to some ticking
she can't quite hear. The awkward silence
has unhinged her life until
it's fallen out-of-joint, a clock
whose hands jump ahead too much.

So she'll slip her fingers into gloves,
just the right ones, the ones
that bring back smells of cinnamon
bread baking on a winter day
and a boy's laughter in the parlor—
the gloves that rein in these lurching hands.

-Lindsey Martin-Bowen

Color of the kitchen

French breakfast puffs
dipped in cinnamon sugar

or cinnamon sugar on toast
for breakfasts at the parents'

at the split level we lived in while I was in grade school
with the linoleum floor in the kitchen
and the cabinets on the west wall

I don't know what color the kitchen was anymore
or how else it was decorated

-Sarah Worrel

Acknowledgments

Sarah Worrel

Sarah would like to thank Lindsey and James for co-writing on this project. She thanks Hannah Jane Weber for her invaluable contribution. Thanks to Frank Robertson for the feedback. Thanks to Jeremey and Teyla for all the advice and hugs. Special thanks go to Spartan Press for giving this work a home.

"I always suspected." Published in *Ravenous and Salivating* (Drone Bee Gazette 2022).

Lindsey Martin-Bowen

Once again, I remain forever grateful to these publishers and editors (excellent, established poets themselves): James Benger and Dan Pohl (Editors of the *365 Days: Poetry Anthology,* now in its 5th volume); Carl Bettis, Nancy Eldridge, Pat Lawson, and Phil Miller (Editors, *The Same*); Gary Lechliter, Maryfrances Wagner, Greg Field (Editors, *I-70 Review*); Brian Daldorph (Editor, *Coal City Review*); Silvia Kofler and Dave Paarmann (Editors/Artistic Directors, *Thorny Locust*); Penny Dunning (Publisher/ Editor, Chatterhouse Press); j.d. tulloch (Publisher/Editor, 39 WEST PRESS); Al Ortolani (Editor, *The Little Balkans Review*); David Memmott (Contributing Editor, *Phantom Drift*). And of course, many thanks to Publisher/Graphic Designer Jason Ryberg and to fellow poets Sarah Worrel and James Benger.

A special thanks to Bob Haynes, Denise Low, Carl Rhoden, long-time poet friends who helped me hone my skills. Likewise, much gratitude to the editors and co-editors who ran my poems in this collection in their anthologies, literary journals, and my previous poetry books:

"It's Never Like the Movies": *Standing on the Edge of the World* (Woodley Press/Washburn U 2008), *Inside Virgil's Garage* (Chatterhouse Books 2013), *The BOOK of FRENZIES* (Pierian Springs Press 2022), and originally in *I-70 Review* (2004).

"Since You Left": *Where Water Meets the Rock* (39 WEST PRESS, 2017). Originally in *Coal City Review* (2014).

"Bonsai Tree Gone Awry": *Inside Virgil's Garage* (Chatterhouse Press 2013).

"September Fires": *365 Days: A Poetry Anthology,* Vol. 4 (2022).

"It Isn't Like the Opera, Either": *The BOOK of FRENZIES* (Pierian Springs Press, 2022) and *365 Days: A Poetry Anthology*, Vol. 4 (2022).

"How You Dull the Pain under this Silent Canopy": *CASHING CHECKS with Jim Morriaon* (redbat books 2023) (original version in *Where Water Meets the Rock* (39 WEST Press 2017) and *Phanthom Drift* (2017)

"Erasures": *CASHING CHECKS with Jim Morrison* (redbat books 2023), originally in I-70 Review (2020).

"County Fair Ferris Wheel Ride": *Porter Gulch Review* (Cabrillo College 2020).

"After Reading 'Saudade" by Erika L. Sanchez": *CASHING CHECKS with Jim Morrison* (redbat books 2023) and originally in *Thorny Locust* (2018).

"Persephone Waits at the Hades Intersection": *The Power of the Feminine*, Vol. I , edited by Christal Ann Rice Cooper and Donna Biffar (Threshpress Midwest 2024); *CASHING CHECKS with Jim Morrison* (redbat books 2023) and originally in *Flint Hills Review* (2018).

"Immortal Beloved": *CASHING CHECKS with Jim Morrison* (redbat books 2023).

"Truckdriver's Wife": *Standing on the Edge of the World* (Woodley Press/Washburn University 2008). Originally published in *New Letters* (Spring 1987, Vol. 53, No.3).

"Mary Todd Lincoln's Obsession": Published in *Inside Virgil's Garage* (Chatter House Press 2013). Originally published in *The Little Balkans Review* (2011).

James Benger

James would like to thank Dan Pohl, Ezhno Martin, Doug Shields, Molly Marjorie, John Dorsey, Victor Clevenger, Maryfrances Wagner, Greg Field, Gary Lechliter, Gay Dust, Tina Hacker, Pat Lawson, Jan Duncan-O'Neal, and Jason Ryberg for giving some of my poems in this collection their first homes, the late Diane Wahto, who's generous spirit and uncompromising tenacity inspired multiple poems in this collection, Alarie Tennile for always supporting my stuff, Sarah Worrel and Lindsey Martin-Bowen for allowing me to tag along on this adventure after most of the heavy lifting had already been done, the members of the 365 Poems in 365 Day group, with whom many of my poems were workshopped, and Dad, Hannah, Milo, and Felix.

"For Diane." Published in *365 Days: A Poetry Anthology,* Volume 3 (2020).

"jackie." Published in *You've Heard It All Before* (2017).

"christmas 1994." Published in *River Dog Zine* (2021).

"chuck taylor's." Published in *I-70 Review* (2022).

"slow inferno." Published in *Ravenous and Salivating* (Drone Bee Gazette 2022).

James Benger has written a bunch of stuff. Some of it has even been published in print and on the interwebs. He is the resident slacker on the Board of Directors of the Writers Place, and is the most truant member of the Riverfront Readings Committee. He is also the admin of an online poetry workshop called 365 Poems in 365 Days, which has produced four anthologies and counting. He lives in Kansas City with his wife and children.

Sarah Worrel works as a paraeducator and is a mother, a video gamer, and a bookworm. She co-authored her first and second books of poetry with James Benger: *Misfits in the Front Row* and *Ravenous and Salivating*. She also writes short stories that have been published in *Coal City Review*, *James Gunn's Ad Astra*, and the anthology *The New Normal*.

Photo by Nelli Sudbrock

On Halloween 2023, redbat books released Lindsey Martin-Bowen's seventh poetry book, *CASHING CHECKS with Jim Morrison.* Her poetry collection, *Where Water Meets the Rock* (39 WEST PRESS 2017) was nominated for a Pulitzer Prize, her *CROSSING KANSAS with Jim Morrison* (in chapbook form) was a semi-finalist in the QuillsEdge Press 2015-2016 Chapbook Contest., and in 2017, it won the Kansas Writers Association award, "Looks Like a Million."

In 2016, Writer's Digest gave her "Vegetable Linguistics" an Honorable Mention in its 85th Annual Contest. Her *Inside Virgil's Garage* (Chatter House Press 2013) was a runner-up in the 2015 Nelson Poetry Book Award, and a poem from it was nominated for a Pushcart Prize. *McClatchy Newspapers/The Kansas City Star* named her *Standing on the Edge of the World* (Woodley Press/Washburn University) one of the Ten Top Poetry Books of 2008. It was nominated for a Pen Award.

Her poems have run in *Contemporary Surrealist* and *Magical Realist Poetry, New Letters, I-70 Review, Thorny Locust, Tittynope Zine, Coal City Review, Amethyst Arsenic, Silver Birch Press, Flint Hills Review, Bare Root Review, The Same, Phantom Drift, Porter Gulch Review, Rockhurst Review,* 21 anthologies, and other literary magazines. She taught at the University of Missouri- Kansas City 18 years, often concurrently at JCCC, MCC -Penn Valley, and MCC-Longview 25 years, and she taught writing, Criminal Law, Criminal Procedure, and American Court Systems (online) for Blue Mountain College in Pendleton, Oregon (2019-2024),. She holds an MA from the University of Missouri and a Juris Doctor degree from the UMKC Law School. While teaching at UMKC and MCCU-Longview, she concurrently taught creative writing, World Literature, and other writing classes at MCCC--Penn Valley for (1993-2005) and Johnson County Community College (1988-2005.)

In a previous life, she was a full-time newspaper reporter for *The Louisville Times* (Louisville, Colorado) and for *The SUN Newspapers* Johnson County, Kansas), an associate editor for *Modern Jeweler Magazine* and the Editor for *The National Paralegal Reporter.*

This project was made possible, in part, by generous support from the Osage Arts Community.

Osage Arts Community provides temporary time, space and support for the creation of new artistic works in a retreat format, serving creative people of all kinds — visual artists, composers, poets, fiction and nonfiction writers. Located on a 152-acre farm in an isolated rural mountainside setting in Central Missouri and bordered by ¾ of a mile of the Gasconade River, OAC provides residencies to those working alone, as well as welcoming collaborative teams, offering living space and workspace in a country environment to emerging and mid-career artists. For more information, visit us at www.osageac.org

Osage Arts Community